Clayton

The Inspirational Story of Baseball Superstar Clayton Kershaw

or abuse of any policies, processes, or directions contained within is the solitary and utter responsibility of the recipient reader. Under no circumstances will any legal responsibility or blame be held against the publisher for any reparation, damages, or monetary loss due to the information herein, either directly or indirectly.

The information herein is offered for informational purposes solely, and is universal as so. The presentation of the information is without contract or any type of guarantee assurance.

The trademarks that are used are without any consent, and the publication of the trademark is without permission or backing by the trademark owner. All trademarks and brands within this book are for clarifying purposes only and are the owned by the owners themselves, not affiliated with this document.

Table Of Contents

Introduction

As the title already implies, this is a short book about [The Inspirational Story of Baseball Superstar Clayton Kershaw] and how he rose from his life in Dallas, Texas to becoming one of today's leading and most-respected baseball players. In his rise to superstardom, Clayton has inspired not only the youth, but fans of all ages, throughout the world.

This book also portrays the key moments that Clayton has had to go through during his early childhood years, his teen years, and up until he became what he is today. A notable source of inspiration is Clayton's service to the community and his strong connection with the fans of the sport. He continues to serve as the humble, hard-working superstar in a sport that needs positive role models.

Combining a filthy curveball, a rife as an arm, high pitching IQ, and superior coordination, Clayton has shown the ability to completely take over a game. From being a small and pudgy adolescent to becoming one of the greatest pitchers of his generation, you'll learn here how this man has risen to the ranks of the best baseball players today.

Thanks again for grabbing this book. Hopefully you can take some of the examples and lessons from Clayton's story and apply them to your own life!

Chapter 1:

Early Childhood & Family Life

Clayton Kershaw was born in Dallas, Texas on March 19th, 1988 to parents, Christopher and Marianne Kershaw. Even when Clayton was a child he already had some large shoes to fill. His great-uncle was an astronomer by the name of Clyde Tombaugh. One of his most notable accomplishments was being known as the man who discovered Pluto. Clayton's mother is the daughter of Clyde's younger brother.

Clayton's father, Christopher, was a musician who won the Clio Award. With such a variety of talent in the blood of his ancestry, Clayton was destined to be something great. Unfortunately, by the age of 10, Clayton's parents had divorced and he went on to be raised by his mother. However, this turn of events led Clayton to become more self-reliant in his youth and grow up quickly. This also led Clayton to become closer to his mother.

Clayton's beginnings as an athlete started when he was first enrolled into youth sports as a child. He played Little League Baseball but was also heavily involved in football and basketball throughout his childhood. Little League Baseball, a three-league non-profit softball and football organization, became the catalyst to why Clayton became such a sporty person.

It also taught him the value of cooperation—and of having a place that made him feel like he "belongs", in one way or another. From then on, Clayton felt like his life mattered—and he was now determined to make his dreams come true.

Chapter 2:

Youth

If you are currently a fan of Clayton, it might be hard to picture Clayton's tall lanky physique as ever being anything else. However, during his youth and early high school career, Clayton was rocking a short and pudgy build. Because of this, he played the center position for the football team. This helped to build a great relationship with his quarterback, who turned out to be famous in his own right. The quarterback who received Clayton's hikes was none other than the Detroit Lions' Matthew Stafford.

The two youngsters hung out with each other's families outside of school and they both were on the same youth football, basketball, soccer, and baseball teams. Not only did these two have the same interests, but they also looked surprisingly similar! Both had similar body structures, hair styles, and were about the same height. They looked so much alike that both of their mothers admitted to having gotten the two confused while cheering for their soccer games. The two boys attended Highland Park High School, and while Matthew was the quarterback of the football team, Clayton played as the center, even dabbling in baseball at the same time.

Eventually, the two played varsity baseball and football together before going on to find success in their respective sports. The amazing thing about their high school success was not the fact that they both were expected to be professional athletes through their endeavors. Rather, it was the fact that most high school baseball scouts saw Clayton as the best high school pitcher in the country and saw Matthew as the top high school quarterback prospect in the country. What are the chances?

While Matthew showed clear promise as a gifted quarterback, showing the ability to throw more than 40 yards before getting to the high school level - a feat that most grown men can not do - it took Clayton a little longer to come into his own. In the summer of his sophomore year, Clayton hit a growth spurt and lost a noticeable amount of weight.

After hitting this unexpected growth spurt, Clayton used his refined pitching repertoire and impressive build to catapult himself into an elite high school prospect. In the year 2006, Clayton posted a 13-0 record with an amazing earned run average of 0.77. To top off his season of excellence, the rapidly developing Clayton recorded 139 strikeouts in only 64 innings pitched.

Through his high school dominance, Clayton also went on to pitch a perfect game - with only strikeouts! In a rare feat for any level of baseball, he took out each of the fifteen hitters he faced via strikeout. It became such a dominant outing that the umpires decided to call an end to the game through the "mercy rule".

At this point, it was obvious that young Clayton had some incredible potential. Not only was the physical feat of this perfect game impressive, but the mental fortitude required to keep composure gave scouts the realization that he could be a top prospect for the Minor Leagues.

To top off his list of high school accomplishments, Clayton was selected as the High School Baseball Player of the Year by USA Today, as well as baseball's Gatorade National Player of the Year award. Clayton also proved that, somehow, he could serve two masters at once—without failing at one of them. He was able to lead his high school football team to victory by setting an incredible 15-0 record.

It should also be noted that Matthew Stafford wasn't Clayton's only childhood friend to make it to the professional ranks. Pitchers Jordan Walden and Shawn Tolleson, who both made it to Major League Baseball, were friends with Clayton before they made it big.

As a side note, Clayton has stated that the reason he wears number 22 is because his favorite player growing up was Will Clark of the Texas Rangers, Clayton's hometown professional team. He and Matthew also continued their friendship, proving that sports, successes, and minute failures could never break up a worthy friendship that had been forged by time.

Chapter 3:

Professional Life

As mentioned earlier, Clayton was widely regarded as the best pitching prospect available for the 2006 Major League Baseball Draft. The Los Angeles Dodgers bought into the hype and took him with the seventh overall pick in the draft.

Prior to the draft, Texas A&M University offered Clayton a full-ride athletic scholarship to attend their school. This had been his plan all along, but being a late bloomer, it was obvious that life had other plans—and they were amazing plans at that. And thus, along with the support of his family, Clayton decided to forego college and pursue a professional baseball career. The fact that the Dodgers also offered him a $2.3 million dollar signing bonus - the largest for any

Dodgers player up until that point - surely helped make the decision a bit easier.

Clayton realized that he would be happier and more productive if he'd accept the deal, and so he did. It also helped that he was unique in his own league. Instead of just being a pitcher, he's a left-handed pitcher—so that ups the ante, and helped him became one of the most respected pitchers around.

Minor League Career

After being drafted by the Dodgers, Clayton began his career with a Little League affiliate of the team, the Gulf Coast League Dodgers. In his time with the affiliate, he struck out 54 batters in only 37 innings. He posted a 2-0 record with an ERA under two.

Soon after, Clayton was promoted to another Dodgers' affiliate, the Great Lakes Loons. He recorded a 7-5 record and a 2.77 ERA. On August 6th, Clayton was promoted to the Jacksonville Suns of Double AA. It was there where he produced a 1–2 record along with a 3.65 ERA in just five starts. He was then brought up to the major leagues for the upcoming season.

In spring training, Clayton received media coverage for throwing a curveball that was so nasty, it began behind the head of Sean Casey and ended up looping back into the strike zone. It was a filthy curve to strike him out. Kershaw was subsequently called up to the Majors, but sent back on July 2nd.

Clayton pitched 18 total innings during his second visit to Jacksonville (one seven inning relief appearance and two starts), winning two games. In this stretch, he allowed just two earned runs, lowering his ERA to 1.91. Clayton was called back up on July 22nd.

Major League Career

First Season_

According to some of the most respected voices in the organization, Clayton's debut was the most anticipated start by a Dodgers pitcher since the 1995 season, when Hideo Nomo made his first major league start. It was on May 25th of 2008 when Clayton made his first start in the majors. He started against the St. Louis Cardinals, striking out the first batter he faced and finished with a total of seven strikeouts. In total, he completed six innings and allowed only two runs. This was definitely a great effort by the young phenom, even more impressive was the fact that Clayton was the youngest player in the entire MLB at the time.

Before long, Clayton won his first game for the Dodgers. It was another six inning outing where he shut out the Nationals, only giving up four hits and totaled five strikeouts. By the end of the season, Clayton finished with a record of 5-5. His ERA was a 4.56 in a total of 22 appearances. Luckily, the Dodgers were able to make the playoffs and Clayton was able to play in the spotlight. He earned an appearance in the 2008 National League Championship Series against the Phillies, although it was out of the bullpen.

Second Season

After a successful rookie season, Clayton showed noticeable improvement in his sophomore campaign. One of his notable games was against the San Francisco Giants, the Dodgers' number one rival, and Clayton delivered for the fans. He struck out thirteen Giants while only giving up one hit. This dominant game put him into historic company, as the only Dodger to strike out thirteen batters in a game since arguably the greatest Dodgers pitcher ever, Sandy Koufax, did so in the 1955 season.

Even though his record wasn't overly impressive, with a final record of 8-8, Clayton led the Majors in hits per nine innings (6.26), opposing slugging percentage (.282), and opposing batting average (.200). He also compiled a total of 185 strikeouts and a notable improvement in ERA from the previous season, with a total of 2.79.

Despite his playoff appearance in the previous postseason, Clayton did not get to make his debut as a starting pitcher. However, in the 2009 postseason, Clayton earned his right to start against the St. Louis Cardinals in the National League Divisional Series. He finished almost 7 innings and earned a no-decision for his outing. It turned out to be a positive result though, as the Dodgers finished the game victorious.

After earning the trust of his manager and teammates, Clayton was named the starter for the opener in the National League Championship Series against Philadelphia. During the previous postseason series with the Phillies, Clayton was not regarded as a dominant ace by any means, rather he was considered to be raw potential. Fast forward a year later, Clayton was the third youngest pitcher to start a playoff series opener. He was clearly coming into his own as a force in the league.

Third Season

Despite Clayton's significant improvement in his first two professional seasons, he still had a glaring weakness - walks. Even through the first month of his third season, Clayton walked 22 hitters during only 29 innings. He had some setbacks where the Dodgers were given a tough chance at victory, including a game against the Brewers, in which he had such a poor outing that he did not even get past the first four outs of the game, being pulled in the second inning.

Despite these setbacks, Clayton pulled himself together, re-focused, and came back stronger than ever. He learned to gain better control of his slider and even went toe-to-toe with Ubaldo Jimenez, in a game in which Clayton pitched a no-hitter through eight innings.

However, Clayton did lose his control in one game where he hit Aaron Rowand of the Giants, in a heated situation where both rival teams were given warnings. Matt Kemp, the Dodgers prime slugger, was hit by Tim Lincecum a few innings earlier in the game, and the umpire viewed Clayton's actions as intentional payback. The result was a five game suspension for Clayton.

Once again, Clayton bounced back from a tough situation, when he faced the Giants in his next outing. He was dominant from beginning to end, finishing the game as a complete game shutout. Clayton's third season was his first one finishing with a record of over .500. He totaled a 13-10 record and an ERA under 3.00. He posted his first season with over 200 innings and 200 strikeouts as well - a sign of him trending into the "elite" category of aces around the league.

Fourth Season: Cy Young Award

By this point in Clayton's young career, most clubs viewed him as one of the top fifteen or so pitchers in the National League. The Dodgers felt the same way, naming him the Opening Day starter for the season. A notable accomplishment was when Clayton pitched back to back complete games, which resulted in victories for his team.

His successful outings did not go unnoticed, as he was awarded the National League Player of the Week award. Clayton's confidence on the diamond seemed to grow each and every week. He was becoming the type of reliable ace that any team would want at the front of their rotation. Not only was his season turning out to be a special one, but he was also setting some legendary benchmarks. He became the youngest pitcher ever to reach 32 career victories to go along with a career ERA of below 3.20, as well as averaging more than a strikeout per inning.

Fans were really starting to ride the Clayton Kershaw bandwagon, shown by the fact that they selected him to the National League All-Star team for the 2011 season. He later won the National League Pitcher of the Month Award for the month of July. By August 23rd, Clayton struck out his 200th batter of the season, becoming the 10th Dodger pitcher to record 200 strikeouts in back-to-back seasons.

To top it all off, Clayton finished the season leading the National League with nearly 250 strikeouts, an ERA of 2.28, and a total of 21 wins - finishing as the National League Triple Crown winner! Many people are familiar with the Triple Crown for hitters but they forget that there is a Triple Crown for pitchers as well.

It is a rare feat that usually involves many factors - both in and out of control of the pitcher who wins it. It involves factors like staying relatively injury-free for the season, being on a team that can score enough runs for you to earn victories, and of course, having absolutely nasty stuff combined with great control.

As if Clayton's amazing season wasn't enough, Justin Verlander, another dominant pitching force, won the Triple Crown award in the American League. This was the first time for such an occurrence since the 1924 season.

Clayton's fielding, something he takes great pride in, also showed improvements from the previous seasons. He was so much better that he won the Gold Glove Award for being the top fielding pitcher in the National League during that season.

Clayton was then awarded the 2011 Warren Spahn Award, presented by the Oklahoma Hall of Fame. This award-giving body is responsible for providing honors to those who are amazing left-handed pitchers—the way Clayton is. Apart from that, he was also given the Most

Outstanding National League Player award from the Players Choice Award, one of the most prestigious recognitions in the world of Baseball, which is voted by baseball players alike, making it all the more special. The prize money that's won by the player would then be donated to charity—definitely a great way of giving back!

The best and biggest recognition he earned that year though, was the National League Cy Young Award. This was introduced way back in 1956 by Ford Frick, the Baseball Commissioner during that time. This award is given to the player who's deemed as Major League Baseball's single best pitcher. Clayton is the youngest person to whom the award has been given, and was the 8th Dodger to be given the same recognition—the last one being Eric Gagne in 2003.

2011 truly proved to be a game-changer not only in the sport, but also in Clayton's own life. It proved that he was someone who is capable of standing up after a big fall - and he surely didn't let the tribulations of his life make him lose hope!

Fifth Season

After Clayton's outstanding 2011 season, he and the Dodgers agreed to a two-year contract extension worth $19 million per year. This made him the second highest earning baseball player. Clayton proved that he had a great standing within the organization, as he was given the distinction as the starter for the Dodgers' on Opening Day.

He finished the season with a league leading ERA of 2.53, a record of 14-9, almost 230 strikeouts, and almost 230 total innings pitched, finishing second in both categories. He also became the first pitcher to lead the league in ERA for consecutive seasons, since Randy Johnson did so for the Arizona Diamondbacks during the 2001-02 seasons.

This was Clayton's fourth year in a row with an ERA of below 3.00, making him the first to do this since Randy Johnson did during 1999–2002. Despite only winning 14 games, Clayton finished second in the National League Cy Young race. He finished behind R.A. Dickey of the New York Mets, but still received two first place votes.

Sixth Season: 2nd Cy Young Award

The 2013 campaign marked the third straight Opening Day start for Clayton. He showed that he was back as a contender for the Cy Young once again, pitching a complete game shutout against the rival Giants. To top it off, he hit a home run in the game as well. He became the first starting pitcher to toss a shutout and hit a homer on Opening Day since the Cleveland Indians' Bob Lemon did it on April 14th of 1953.

Before long, Clayton notched his 1,000th career strikeout on April 17th, after striking out Yonder Alonso of the San Diego Padres. Soon after, Clayton surpassed the mark of 1,000 total innings pitched for his career.

Clayton finished the season with a total of 16 wins, over 230 innings pitched, and a Major League best of 0.92 WHIP and 1.83 ERA. Not only was he only the third pitcher to lead the Major Leagues in ERA for three years in a row, but he showed that his weakness when he came into the league, which was walking too many batters, was now one of his strengths. His control and composure was becoming one of his better assets.

It was almost a no-brainer for Clayton to receive the American League Cy Young award after one of the most dominant seasons by a pitcher in recent memory. He won the award for the second time in three seasons and cemented his place as one of the best pitchers in the game.

Unsurprisingly, the Dodgers were going to do whatever they could in order to keep Clayton as their long-term ace. He agreed to an extension worth $215 million over the span of seven years. The deal marked the biggest in the history of MLB for a starting pitcher. Even Justin Verlander, arguably the only other pitcher who could rival Clayton as the league's top ace, was "only" signed to a contract of seven years and

$180 million. Of course it helped that the Los Angeles Dodgers have a history of not being afraid to spend money on players they value.

Seventh Season

Clayton ran into some unfortunate back injury issues early on in his 2014 season, he was eventually placed on the disabled list for the first time in his career. It took until May before he was able to rejoin the team at full health. However, before long he was back to typical Clayton.

In an amazing feat, Clayton threw a complete game no-hitter against the Rockies. Not only that, he struck out fifteen batters in the game, a career high for him. Furthermore, there was only one player who reached base in the game, and that was due to an error. This meant that he was only an error away from a perfect game!

He won the Pitcher of the Month Award for June after posting an incredible 0.82 ERA to go along with a 6-0 record. To get to these numbers,

Clayton had a streak of 41 innings where he did not allow a single run. He won the Pitcher of the Month Award again for the month of July, showing the world that his injury was not going to hamper him.

Clayton completed the season with a total record of 21-3 and his ERA was his best yet, at a measly 1.77. To top it all off, he led the National League in almost every single relevant statistic that is important for a starting pitcher. It also should be noted that he did all of this despite missing most of the first month of the season.

Clayton was finally alone in the history books, becoming the only pitcher in the history of Major League Baseball to lead the league in ERA for four consecutive seasons. A wide variety of baseball analysts regarded his 2014 season as one of the greatest by a pitcher in the last few decades.

He became one of the most notable and most awarded players during this season. Baseball America and the Sporting News named him as the Player of the Year. Apart from that, he was given the distinction as the Outstanding NL Pitcher from the Players Choice Awards. He was also given the Marvin Miller Man of the Year Award, an award given to baseball players who have given amazing on-field contributions and performances to the community, having been presented by Mark McGwire, a former professional Baseball Player.

Eighth Season

In the following year, Clayton was given the honor of being the Opening Day starter once again, and had the chance to get his 1,500th inning against the Colorado Rockies. On May 15th of that year, he was able to gain another career win - the 100th of his career, and even became the second youngest active pitcher, and 22nd pitcher in history to get those 100 wins. He also gained another Player of the Week Distinction after striking out 18 hitters, doing so in 15 innings.

However, it seemed as if Clayton's fame waned a bit, as surprisingly, he did not make the initial National League roster for the All Star Game. But, he was still able to join the game as a replacement for pitcher Max Scherzer, who could not pitch on that day. Of course, it was a bit of a blow to the ego, but still, Clayton proved that even if he was just a replacement, he surely was a great player. And guess what? He became that game's best pitcher!

Later that season, he recorded his 200th strikeout, being the fastest one to do so - in 156 innings at that!

Ninth Season

In 2016, Clayton was able to make the Opening Day lineup again, and he won 6 straight games to start off the campaign. He even set a record of games with 10 strikeouts or more without more than 1 hit or walk - the lowest in all of the modern era.

However, in an unfortunate series of events, Clayton had to be placed on the disabled list at the end of June due to lingering back pain, and was unable to pitch in the All-Star Game. By August, he was placed on the 60-day disabled list.

It may have been a tumultuous year for Clayton, but knowing him, it just might be sooner rather than later before he makes his way back up to the top!

Chapter 4:

Personal Adult Life

Off the field, Clayton happily married his girlfriend of seven years, Ellen, on December 4th, 2010. Their relationship started in the ninth grade, when Clayton stopped Ellen Melson in the five minutes between classes and asked her to go on a date with him. Ellen said yes, and Clayton headed off to lunch.

Their first dates involved doing homework on Ellen's kitchen table, where she helped him with his art sketches and Clayton helped her with her math homework. Before long, Clayton found himself in the middle of a large and welcoming family. From that point on, Clayton and Ellen have been going strong as a couple.

After he and Ellen were married in 2010, Clayton began to take interest in her passion for helping others and it has become a big factor in his life. In addition to his relationship with Ellen, Clayton is also publicly proud of his Methodist faith and claims to be a strong follower of the religion.

For fun, Clayton made a cameo appearance in the third season of "New Girl", which aired following FOX's showing of Super Bowl XLVIII.

Being An Author

Clayton's wide variety of interests also include writing and being a creative mind. He and his wife, Ellen, co-authored a book named "Arise: Live Out Your Faith and Dreams on Whatever Field You Find Yourself", a book about their Christian faith and humanitarian efforts. The book was released on January 5th, 2012, through Regal Press.

The fact that Clayton is so proud to express his beliefs is what causes people to look up to him, especially the youth trying to find their way. He is certainly a stand-out among the common man, both physically and mentally.

Chapter 5:

Philanthropic/Charitable Acts

Many people are so focused on his on-field accomplishments that they are unaware of Clayton's charitable acts off the baseball field.

For the last few years, Clayton has been holding an annual ping-pong charity event. The proceeds from his event, "Ping Pong 4 Purpose" go directly to benefit Clayton's foundation, "Kershaw's Challenge".

"Kershaw's Challenge" is an organization that uses Christ as its guidance and serves to benefit children's charities in the Dallas area, Los Angeles area, and in Africa. In effect, it focuses on providing opportunities to children in underprivileged communities who wouldn't

otherwise get those resources - certainly a noble
cause.

Humanitarian Work

Prior to the 2011 campaign, Clayton made a visit to Zambia along with his wife, as part of a Dallas-based organization Christian mission, called Arise Africa.

After being moved by what he saw during this trip, Clayton announced his vision of building an orphanage in Lusaka, a crown in Zambia. Clayton called the project "Hope's Home", inspired by an eleven year old girl named Hope, a child who was diagnosed as HIV-positive.

To reach this goal, Clayton committed to donating $100 per strikeout in 2011 - a bold statement for a man who strikes batters out in his sleep! Not surprisingly, Clayton recorded his career high of 248 strikeouts in that season and it resulted in a very impactful donation to the cause.

Furthermore, in the past four off-seasons, Clayton and his wife have worked to construct a home, a school, and build water wells in the area. Clayton is not satisfied with just writing checks, he actually wants some control in the execution of he and Ellen's vision. The fact that he gets his hands dirty, even with all of his professional acclaim, is certainly commendable. After all, those hands earn him a lot of money in his day job.

As well as Kershaw's Challenge and Hope's Home, Clayton has also helped with other causes in the Los Angeles area, including helping Habitat for Humanity rehabilitate and demolish a home in Lynwood, California. Clayton is also a supporter of the Peacock Foundation, an organization that supplies animal-assisted actions and interventions for the youth that is at risk. It does this by partnering with community organizations, public service agencies, and mental health professionals.

Being in Zambia truly opened up Clayton's eyes to the harsh realities of the world. He realized that life isn't just about baseball, football, or other sports - it is so much more than that. All of his triumphs almost made him forget about what life really is about, and for him, the Zambia trip was sort of like a wake-up call that he most definitely needed.

It also showed how Clayton has such kindness in his heart, prompting him to do whatever he can to help save more lives. It also prompted him to work even better in the league, because he already saw the world for what it is, and he's no longer blinded by just what's beautiful or great.

Clayton made such an impact with his humanitarian work that he was awarded the Roberto Clemente Award for the 2012 season. He also received the Branch Rickey Award in 2013 as recognition for his outstanding work in community service.

Chapter 6:

Legacy, Potential & Inspiration

Clayton Kershaw is known for his attention to detail, work ethic, and sense of control when it comes to preparation. Even at a young age, Clayton showed that he would control what was in his power. As a child of a single mother, Clayton made sure he did his homework and housework on time, before going out to play with his friends.

Despite all of his massive success as a professional athlete, Clayton has shown great loyalty. He has maintained his same group of core friends from his childhood. No amount of money will make him turn his back on the people who love him - something that can't be said about all superstar athletes.

Another attractive aspect of Clayton's personality is his ability to stick with his word and not take everything too seriously. He clearly has a light-hearted approach to fans and media, not focused on crafting a squeaky-clean image that is not accessible to the masses. He interacts with media types and interviewers with the same type of respect as someone who is struggling just to make the minor leagues, even though he is a multiple time Cy Young award winner.

Most notably, Clayton is an easy guy to hang around with in the clubhouse. Many of his teammates have noted that he takes jokes well and doesn't take criticism - or praise - personally. He takes it all in stride as part of the job.

He is a great example of a person showing that you do not need to conform to a predetermined mold after becoming successful in your field of work. From the words of his little league and high school coaches, to his minor league and major league coaches, you will be hard-pressed to find instances in which Clayton thought he was bigger than the team.

His desire for input and control makes the game easier for catchers, the defensive players behind him, and his coaches as well. Because he wants as much input as possible, players are more than willing to follow in line. He will blame himself if another person makes a mistake, take responsibility for an error made by an infielder, and give his honest opinion to a coach or to his catcher without worrying about hurting feelings.

Clayton's peers have often said that he is a perfectionist. His teammate AJ Ellis has a profound memory of Clayton warming up - three fastballs in the middle - but he just did not stop there. Instead, he was able to do three more fastballs on each side, with the right changeups after, and then three curveballs to the middle - all with the exact same mechanics and motion. He would then go to the "stretch" position, and would do two to five fastballs inside, then out, another two curveballs, two sliders, a windup, fastball, and then sliders again. He would end up with 34 pitches. He would do all these without looking or feeling tired - and without looking as if he was exhausted.

According to Ellis, it was one of those things that he admired about Clayton: he was such a perfectionist, but for good reason. He wanted to do his best not only for himself, but also for his team. After facing setbacks in the past, he was determined to earn his way up - not the easy way around, but by really doing his best in whatever way he could. Not a lot of players have that drive and determination, especially after being given many accolades.

As noted by many of the top scouts in the game, Clayton's pitching style relies a great deal on deception. He is great at hiding the ball so that hitters are not able to predict what is coming next. Out of the stretch, especially being a left-handed pitcher, he uses his slide step so that runners at first are less likely to test him. Furthermore, his pick-off move is considered to be one of the best in the game. He has even stated that he patterned this off of Roger Clemens, even though Clemens was a right-handed thrower.

Of course, his back issues are always a potential problem - especially now. Clayton knows he could be replaced anytime. It happens in life. Heck, he was not even part of the All-Star Game, but instead of wallowing in his sorrows, he's able to motivate himself to rise back up, be part of that elite group again, still continue doing his best.

He is the kind of person who's not going to be put down just by the negative stuff that's happening. He makes sure to it that he gets motivated by them—and that he sees the world both as his playground, and as a place where he could do so much for - a place where he could show what he's about, and be able to help others out in the process, as well.

Clayton's career may currently be on hold, but 2016 still isn't over. There are four more months ahead, and in those months, Clayton may return back to the game. If not, there's always next year. But whatever happens, Clayton has already proved that he is truly a force to be reckoned with in the line of baseball, and he's not just "another player".

From growing up without a father, to realizing what he's meant for in high school, and on to his colorful career in the Minor, Major, and National Leagues, Clayton has proved that he's the one to beat - but without taking it to his head, he remained humble, still has a lot of passion for the game, and truly has proven to be one of the most inspiring and important people in the sport of baseball.

One can only hope to emulate and be more like him.

Conclusion

Hopefully this book was able to help you gain inspiration from the life of Clayton Kershaw, one of the best players currently playing in Major League Baseball.

The rise and fall of a star is often the cause for much wonder. But most stars have an expiration date. In baseball, once a star player reaches his mid- to late-thirties, it is often time to contemplate retirement. What will be left in people's minds about that fading star? In Clayton Kershaw's case, people will remember how he came onto the scene for the Dodgers and helped to form one of the best pitching rotations in franchise history. He will be remembered as the guy who helped his team build their image in their journey back to the World Series, while building his own image along the way.

Quiet, laid-back, and shy, this Los Angeles Dodgers pitcher has baseball fans in awe with a playing prowess that sportswriters say is comparable to that of the legendary, Sandy Koufax. Coupled with a light-hearted attitude, superior attention to detail and preparation, and a boy-next-door smile, he's baseball card material for sure.

Clayton has also inspired so many people because he is the star who never fails to connect with fans and gives back to the less fortunate. Noted for his ability to impose his will on any game, he is a joy to watch on the baseball field. Last but not least, he's remarkable for remaining simple and firm with his principles in spite of his immense popularity.

Hopefully you learned some great things about Clayton in this book and are able to apply some of the lessons that you've learned to your own life! Good luck in your journey!

CPSIA information can be obtained
at www.ICGtesting.com
Printed in the USA
LVHW081401310820
664650LV00014B/509

9 781508 435617